Original title:
Thorn-Covered Tales

Copyright © 2025 Creative Arts Management OÜ
All rights reserved.

Author: Lila Davenport
ISBN HARDBACK: 978-1-80567-049-0
ISBN PAPERBACK: 978-1-80567-129-9

Stories Woven with Prickles

In a garden where the roses plot,
A cunning hare forgot his spot.
He danced on blooms as thorns did stare,
While giggling bees buzzed without a care.

A clever cat with whiskers sharp,
Played the lute, a hidden harp.
But every tune got pricked, oh dear,
The notes flew off, like startled deer.

Secrets in the Shadowed Grove

In the woods where shadows creep,
The squirrels gather secrets to keep.
They chuckle low, with acorns harmed,\nAs breezes
through the branches charmed.

A raccoon's mask hides cheeky grins,
While each tale told, the laughter spins.
With every twist, the prickle's found,
In this grove where giggles abound.

Whispers from the Wild Briars

Amidst the brambles, whispers flow,
A crafty fox puts on a show.
He jests and jives, but oh, beware,
For hidden thorns tag him with flair.

The rabbits laugh, the birds all tweet,
As he stumbles on his clumsy feet.
Each playful hop, a thorny chase,
Turns into fun—a wild embrace.

Petals and Pains

The flowers bloom with vibrant pride,
But hidden sharpness, they can't hide.
A clumsy snail crawls with great flair,
  And leaves behind a thorny scare.

The daisies giggle, swaying free,
  While prickly humor's the key.
From every poke and every sting,
Comes laughter, joy—oh, what a fling!

Beauty Amidst the Bramble

In a patch where roses weave,
A squirrel finds a treasure sleeve.
With prickles all around him there,
He chases dreams without a care.

A ladybug in polka dots,
Waltzes through the tangled knots.
With each misstep, a giggle bleeds,
As laughter blooms from funny weeds.

When bushes wear a spiky crown,
The bunnies hop without a frown.
They nibble snacks and jump with glee,
While dodging branches, wild and free.

Yet through the mess, a joke unfolds,
For every prick, a story told.
In nature's laughter, we find grace,
Chasing joy in bulging space.

The Weighted Thorn

Once a rose named Prickly Sue,
Claimed she'd win a beauty due.
Yet every time she seemed to glow,
Her thorns would steal the wondrous show.

A bee came by, he was quite bold,
He laughed as Sue grew stiff and cold.
He danced around her prickly pride,
And whispered, "Girl, just take a ride!"

With bloated bees and clumsy feet,
The garden turned into a feat.
Prickly Sue learned to embrace,
Her weighted thorns with funny grace.

So if you stroll by bramble vine,
Remember laughter's sweet design.
For even when the thorns are near,
A chuckle's worth a grand frontier.

A Story Told by Stingers

In a garden full of stings,
A bumblebee with laughter sings.
He buzzes tales of prickled plight,
Making every gloom feel light.

"Come hear my story," he declares,
Of stingers proud and knotted hairs.
Each thorny twist, a punchline spun,
As flowers nod and join the fun.

A ladybug, she joins the cheer,
With jokes about her polka rear.
While catkins sway, they laugh away,
The burdens of a spiky day.

So when you feel a sting unfold,
Just think of stories sweetly told.
For in the bramble, joy can thrive,
With laughter buzzing, we survive.

Tales of Resilience Amidst the Rough

In the midst of bramble snag,
There blooms a rose without a flag.
"Why so serious?" the thorns demand,
As they tickle dreams and play a hand.

Each prickle brings a giggle round,
As critters dance upon the ground.
With every poke, there's laughter shared,
In this wild garden unprepared.

A hedgehog slips, but what a show,
He bounces back, kicks up the dough.
With every thorn, a punchline waits,
In nature's court of funny fates.

So let the brambles grow and twist,
Embrace the fun, make memories gist.
For in resilience, humor grows,
In tangled tales where laughter flows.

Fragments of a Barbed Dream

In the garden of laughter, I stumble and trip,
Where daisies wear armor, adorned with a quip.
Chasing a dream that pricks like a rose,
With each tiny jab, I can't help but doze.

Bumbling through blossoms, I dance with delight,
Dodging sharp whispers that tease in the night.
Petals seem to giggle, their secrets they keep,
While I juggle my worries in a prickly heap.

Tickling the blooms with my clumsy hands,
Falling for fairest, that no one understands.
In a mess of my making, I can't quite explain,
Why I love this misfit in gorgeous disdain.

Between Beauty and Pain

A butterfly lands on a critter of pricks,
Sipping nectar while playing its tricks.
Oh, what a scenario, tragic and sweet,
The charming offense is hard to compete.

Among velvet petals, a sly smile is found,
Where chaos and beauty spin round and round.
A bee with bold swagger buzzes by near,
Claiming the flower, shrugging in cheer.

Yet lurking beneath are the thorns of the jest,
Inviting all suckers to join in the fest.
With laughter like sunlight, our worries disperse,
In this blooming disaster, we all sing in verse.

The Struggle to Bloom

Once a seed in the dirt, dreaming big dreams,
I reached for the sky with my leaf-covered schemes.
Trying so hard to break through the soil,
But my armor of thorns made my efforts recoil.

With a flourish of humor, I sought to offend,
Nature's odd choices, I can't quite defend.
Each poke and embarrassment, I tucked in my sleeve,
While my neighbor, a rose, just mocked and believed.

Through the laughter and jabs, I found my own place,
In the garden of folly, I'm winning the race.
Braving the barbs in this comical plight,
I bloom in eccentricity, what a delight!

Shadows in the Garden

In the shadows, the veggies are whispering tales,
About weeds full of mischief, sneaking like snails.
Each cucumber chuckles at radishes' fate,
While carrots just roll their eyes, irate.

A gnome in the corner, with paint on his hat,
Tries to keep order while laughing at that.
The laughter erupts from the peppers and beans,
Dancing to rhythms, they whisper their dreams.

But beware the surprises lurking below,
For the tricks of a garden come with a show.
As jokes bloom and fester in curious spots,
I grin through the chaos, the punchlines are hot.

Resilience of the Wildflower

In cracks of concrete, wildflowers sprout,
They giggle at weeds, dancing about.
With roots so stubborn, they stand so tall,
Claiming the pavement, they conquer all.

When raindrops fall, they leap with glee,
Sipping the sweet drops, as spry as can be.
With petals that flutter and colors so bright,
They wear their beauty like a dazzling light.

In the Weeds of our Tales

In tangled stories, laughter grows wide,
With roots intertwining, we twist, we glide.
The punchlines hidden beneath leafy beds,
We dig for the humor in all that it spreads.

Each tale's a tangle, where giggles may hide,
With thorns that poke gently, but joy is the guide.
Through all the mess, there lies a fair jest,
Joy blooms in chaos, it really is best.

Beauty's Barbed Whispers

Whispers of beauty, wrapped tight in brambles,
They tickle our cheeks and prompt little rambles.
A prick here and there lends a playful tease,
While the blossoms above dance in the breeze.

With colors that charm and laughter that sings,
Beauty can pack quite the punch with sharp flings.
Beneath all the ruckus, a joke's gently told,
In the wild of the garden, pure humor unfolds.

The Weight of Rooted Secrets

Secrets lie deep in the soil so thick,
Beneath tangled roots, they play their slick trick.
With each playful rustle, a secret takes flight,
As blooms burst with laughter, they'll conquer the night.

The weight of the tales buried deep underground,
Who knew that old mumbles could make such a sound?
Yet in every giggle, resilience shines bright,
In the weight of our roots, it's laughter we write.

Complications Beneath the Flowers

In a garden lush and bright,
Bees buzzed with all their might.
Yet every bloom, a prickly joke,
Brought laughter with each poke.

Roses wore their thorns with pride,
While daisies whispered, "Come inside!"
The tulips giggled, feeling bold,
As prickers made their stories told.

A daffodil in sunlit cheer,
Exclaimed, "Don't come too near!"
For every bloom that smiles and beams,
A hidden thorn is in our dreams.

So in this patch, where blooms abound,
It's not just beauty that we've found.
For laughter hides in every cut,
And roses know how to strut!

Strength in the Sharp Shadows

In shadows where the roses grow,
A rough and tumble garden show.
Petals soft, but oh so sly,
With prickers aimed to make you cry.

Daisies chase the bees away,
While tulips plot for their grand play.
"Don't touch us!" is their cheeky chant,
As spiders try to weave and plant.

They laugh at cautious, wandering feet,
For every bloom, a prickly greet.
With colors bright and wits so keen,
In the shadow, the thorns are seen.

So take your time, but do beware,
This garden's got its funny flair.
With blooms that sprout and laughter born,
Behind their petals, lies the thorn.

Whirls of Nature's Irony

In sunlit fields, the bumbles thrived,
While prickly plants slyly connived.
Every petal turned to glee,
Hiding sharpness, tough as can be.

A dandelion learned to dance,
While thorns made all the plants enhance.
"What a twist!" the daisies sighed,
As prickles formed a guard so wide.

Laughter echoed through the trees,
As critters teased the buzzing bees.
Nature's jesters, sharp and bright,
In every bloom, a quirky bite.

So join the frolic, take a chance,
In gardens where the petals prance.
For nature's tales are funny, true,
With hidden laughs, just waiting for you!

Petals That Protect

Underneath the gentle blooms,
Lurked whispers laced with silly dooms.
"Come closer!" mocked the puffy rose,
While poky thorns hid in a pose.

A sunflower tried to keep it cool,
But thorns made it a prickly fool.
With petals bright and jokes on tap,
All nature wore a giggly cap.

The violets laughed at every tick,
As thorns adorned their playful trick.
"What good is beauty if it can't tease?"
In garden realms, the blooms all squeeze.

So frolic through this petal play,
Where laughter sharpens every day.
With protectors in silly rows,
In every petal, humor grows!

Tales from a Twisted Vines

In a garden where the weeds do waltz,
Laughter rises, who knows the faults?
Vines twist and twirl like dancers rare,
Each leaf whispers secrets, a funny affair.

A snail wearing glasses takes his slow stroll,
Chasing the sun like a playful goal.
The roots plot mischief, all in good cheer,
While the daisies giggle, it's clear they're near.

A frog sings operas from a shady nook,
While the grasshoppers laugh, giving him the hook.
Among tangled whispers and leafy quips,
Even the bugs are doing backflips!

So join the party where oddities play,
Underneath laughter, we chase woes away.
In this wild garden, full of delight,
Every twist tells a story that's out of sight!

Unspoken Words Underneath Spikes

Underneath the spikes, secrets shy,
A squirrel clutches acorns and winks an eye.
The shadows giggle as they twist and turn,
While the roses plot, let's watch and learn.

A cactus tells tales with a prickly laugh,
While the daisies roll on the grass for a gaff.
Whispers float by on a breeze quite bold,
Crafting mischief that never gets old.

A hedgehog critiques, with a snorting glee,
The way the fox dances beneath the old tree.
Every branch holds a chuckle, every vine a grin,
As nature's oddities spin tales that win!

So hear the quiet chuckles held so tight,
Amongst the pointed leaves, there's sweet delight.
For every unspoken word rings with cheer,
In the land of prickers, we shed every fear!

Barbs of Memory

Memories stick like burrs on a sock,
Their prickly touch makes everyone gawk.
With each little poke, there's laughter to find,
In the mishaps we treasure, oh so unrefined.

A gnome tipped over with a wobble and spin,
While the flowers are laughing, it's hard not to grin.
A squirrel with style, sporting a cap,
Turns every blunder into a fun mishap.

Dancing through recollections, the good and the strange,
Every twist and turn is part of the change.
So let the barbs of our past tickle our feet,
And step on the paths where humor's a treat!

As we stroll through the gardens of folly and cheer,
Collecting the memories, both far and near.
With laughter as our armor, we bound and we soar,
Embracing each moment, who could ask for more?

The Rose's Secret Veil

Behind the petals, the rose hides away,
Whispering giggles at the end of the day.
With a secret veil and a wink so sly,
It welcomes the bees with a mischievous sigh.

In the corners where shadows cast a fun spell,
The daisies hold meetings, oh what tales they tell!
A ladybug's gossip and a caterpillar's tease,
Bring laughter and joy, and a soft, gentle breeze.

The thorns play guardians of whimsy and jest,
Every poke brings humor; it's put to the test.
For in every bloom lies a prankster's delight,
Sparkling joy under the golden daylight.

So raise your glass to the laughter we share,
Where secrets hide under sweet, fragrant air.
In this garden of giggles, let's dance and unveil,
The hilarity wrapped in a rose's sweet tale!

Between the Pricks of Passion

In a garden vast and bright,
A bee buzzed with all his might.
He tripped on blooms, oh what a sight,
His love for roses was pure delight.

But oh, the petals hid a scheme,
A love that clutched like a bad dream.
The thorns took aim, or so it seemed,
And made his heart scream with a meme!

Inside the Tightly Wrapped Buds

A bud was snug as a bug in a rug,
Hiding secrets, feeling a tug.
With every twist, it gave a shrug,
And plotted how to spring a hug.

Yet when the sun shone bright with glee,
It popped open, set itself free.
It shouted 'Look at me, whee!'
And pricked a friend, oh dearie me!

Whirling Through Nature's Thorns

A squirrel danced through tangled vines,
With acorn dreams and silly signs.
He spun and twirled, forgot the lines,
Until he learned life's thorny fines.

He slipped on petals, then fell down,
Flipping his bushy tail, he frowned.
"Who knew the stroll would wear a crown?"
But up he got, still nature-bound!

Lessons in the Overgrowth

In jungles thick, where shadows play,
A wise old tortoise lost his way.
He learned to laugh at every stay,
And waved to thorns, 'What's here today?'

A rabbit hopped, so spry and fast,
'Slow down, my friend, make moments last!'
But thorns gave chase; a lesson cast,
In overgrowth, giggles amassed!

The Gentle Caress of Pain

A prick to remind me, oh what a tease,
The flowers around me just laugh with ease.
I dance through the garden, my feet all a-flare,
Yet each gentle step leaves me gasping for air.

Oh, sweet irony, joy wrapped in woe,
A tickling humor, where chaos does flow.
I giggle and stumble, my heart full of cheer,
As I trip on the petals that bite like a spear.

In the Thicket of Dreams

In a forest of thoughts where the wild things roam,
I found a lost shoe and a sad little gnome.
He said, 'Watch your step, it's a whimsical place,
The brambles are friendly, but give you a chase!'

A branch waved hello, it was silly, I swear,
While whispers of laughter filled up the cold air.
I chased after giggles, got stuck in a mess,
But who knew the thicket could cause such distress?

Uprooted Yet Blooming

I'm a flower that bloomed from a tenuous grip,
A pot full of dirt and a wild little sip.
My roots pulled and tugged, they chuckled aloud,
'You think you are special? Just roll with the crowd!'

With colors so bright but a stem full of fray,
I wobble and sway in a lovable way.
Each petal a story with laughter in folds,
A comedy show where the punchline unfolds.

Hidden Threads of Barbed Memory

In the attic of memories, cobwebs do cling,
I found my old jokes, oh the joy that they bring!
Each thread, a reminder, with a playful sting,
I laugh 'til I cry at their sharp little zing.

A tapestry woven with color and pain,
Where giggles get lost in a tangled refrain.
Yet in every snag, there's a chuckle I find,
With the barbs of the past, oh what fun they unwind!

The Serenade of Spiny Stems

Oh, dance around the bristle bush,
With prickly thoughts and a silly rush.
The flowers laugh as we carefully tread,
Poking our legs, that's where we dread!

The moonlight flickers on jagged leaves,
We're dressed in laughter, oh what a tease!
A waltz with thorns can be quite a sight,
As we stumble forward, all filled with fright!

The critters giggle from their leafy lair,
As we trip and tumble, without a care.
A concerto of edges, a symphony bold,
With every misstep, our tales unfold!

So here's to the spiky, the fun, and the strange,
In a garden where humor can always arrange.
Let's sing to the brambles and joke with the blooms,
In this wacky place, no one ever grooms!

Cuando el Amor se Cubre

En un jardín lleno de espinas,
El amor desfila con grandes rimas.
Se tropieza un poco, se ríe de a montón,
Mientras acaricia con su corazón.

Las risas surgen tras cada pinchazo,
Un baileteo en el amarillo abrazo.
Las mariposas vuelan, todas risueñas,
Cruzando los miedos, dejando las señas.

Hasta el sol se asoma, con miradas curiosas,
Sintiendo los saltos de almas ansiosas.
Un beso entre hojas puede causar confusión,
Pero la locura es pura diversión.

Y al final de la danza, todos nos reímos,
Entre espinas y amores, siempre nos entendemos.
Así que, ven querido, no te resistas,
Brindemos por espinas y por risas tan vistas!

Tales from the Edges of Existence

In a land where giggles meet sharp demise,
Stories unfold beneath the skies.
We tiptoe on edges where cactus blooms,
And laughter erupts in the spiky rooms.

A hedgehog's tale of a wild chase,
With bumps and bruises, still keeping grace.
The snickers of critters from their leafy nooks,
Integration of laughter hides in the crooks.

Once a bee stumbled, looking for nectar,
Found more than he bargained, a thorny sector.
With a buzz and a glow, he lost his way,
Now he's the town joke, sunny all day!

So gather the stories from the edges wide,
Where humor and sharpness take us for a ride.
In this land of tickles and wise old fables,
We dance through the prickers and laugh while we're able!

Grit Between Grace

In a garden where laughter grows,
A clumsy bee trips on his toes.
With honey dreams and buzzing plans,
He lands in dirt, not in the cans.

The flowers giggle, petals sway,
As he stumbles on his merry way.
Grace couldn't save him from the muck,
Yet he buzzes on, just out of luck.

A ladybug calls, 'What's the fuss?'
'Oh, I'm just a bee, no need to cuss!'
With grit between his regal dance,
He twirls in soil, not taking a chance.

So next time you trip on the ground,
Remember that laughter can always be found.
In life's little stumbles, there's a funny grace,
Just like our bee, wear a smile on your face.

Shattered Petal Dreams

A dainty bud dreamed of the sky,
But found herself in a pastry pie.
A baker's hand, oh what a plight,
Flour-dusted dreams are quite the sight!

'I'm meant for beauty!' the petal cried,
Yet on a tart, she must abide.
With whipped cream clouds, oh what a scene,
Life's kitchen can be so very mean!

A cheeky squirrel came for a taste,
He giggled aloud, wasn't it a waste?
Shattered dreams in a sea of cream,
Life's a dessert, or so it would seem.

But every crumble brings laughter too,
Even blossoms caught in a bake-off brew.
For in each slice of life's keen schemes,
There's joy found even in shattered dreams.

A Symphony of Sharp Edges

In the orchestra of life's sharp notes,
A cactus strummed with prickly coats.
His spines resonated a tune so bold,
While clumsy musicians tried to hold.

A hedgehog tapped on his spiky back,
"Hey, dear cacti, don't lose your knack!"
With kerfuffle near the woodwind section,
They bumbled 'round in keen connection.

The clarinet squeaked; the flute went 'ping!'
While sights of chaos danced in spring.
"Just stick to it," the cactus cheered,
For jolly tunes are best when weird!

So let us all play our parts with pride,
Even if our edges sometimes collide.
In the symphony of life, just engage,
Laughing through each sharp-edged stage.

The Splendor in the Scratches

In a field where daisies seem to fight,
A kitty pranced with all her might.
But oops! A branch caught her fluffy tail,
As she danced and stumbled, oh what a tale!

'A scratch for flair!' cried her furry friend,
'We wear our battles like a badge to send.'
Through the wildflowers, their giggles flew,
Pouncing and prancing, oh what a view!

Scratches and giggles, oh what a mix,
In the land of joy, they pull their tricks.
A tumble here, a sparkle there,
In the splendor of mishaps, they joyfully share.

So when you find yourself in a scrape,
Just laugh it out; there's always an escape.
For scratches, my friend, can lead to delight,
In life's wild dance, it's all done in light.

A Journey Through the Brambles

In a patch of prickles, we tripped and we fell,
Laughed at the chaos, oh what a tale to tell.
Bumbled through bushes, socks full of leaves,
Who knew adventure could come with such thieves?

Brambles were waving, like hands in a crowd,
Taunting our journey, both silly and loud.
We dodged and we weaved like a dance through the thorns,
While giggling at life, through a chorus of scorns.

The berries were juicy, red as a clown's nose,
We feasted on fruits, 'till our laughter arose.
Our trails were a maze, and our giggles the map,
A journey so wild, we both took a nap!

So here's to the brambles, our friends in mischief,
Making mundane moments feel like a gift.
With every sharp poke, we smiled a bit more,
In a world full of pricks, we opened the door.

Resilience in Bloom

A little flower blooms in a patch of despair,
Surrounded by barbs, but it doesn't care.
It sways in the breeze, like it knows the truth,
Telling the thorns, 'I'm your funny little sleuth!'

With petals a-swish, it's quite a surprise,
Winning its battle with tenacious ties.
The pinching and poking, it giggles and jest,
Dancing through prickles, it's truly the best!

Each thorn is a joke, every scratch is a pun,
This flower's a comedian, oh, isn't it fun?
It stands tall and proud, in colors so bright,
Defying the odds, like a star in the night.

So let's raise a toast to the blooms we can see,
For standing through prickles, they thrive wild and free.
A lesson in laughter, all wrapped in a crown,
In a patch full of barbs, it won't ever frown!

The Barbs of Yesterday

Once I took a stroll down a memory lane,
Where barbs poked my heart, oh what a strange pain.
I laughed at the moments, so sharp but so sweet,
Funny how heartache can dance on your feet!

Those pricks of the past, they tickled my mind,
Each memory a giggle, so easy to find.
I stumbled and fumbled, with grace like a seal,
Yet here I am laughing, at the way that I feel.

Woes wrapped in humor, oh what a delight,
Transforming old barbs into laughs late at night.
I share tales of woe, with a wink and a grin,
For each prick reminds me where I've been.

So here's to the moments, both silly and bright,
With barbs in the past, we'll dance through the light.
The scars tell our stories, so let's raise a cheer,
To the tales that once hurt, now bring us a leer!

The Vicious Embrace

There once was a hug from a friend so sincere,
It felt like a cuddle, but packed quite a spear.
A poke here, a jab there, a laughter-filled mess,
Who knew a warm hug could be such a stress?

They wrapped me in joy with their wild, flailing arms,
But little did I know I'd be met with such charms.
We laughed and we squealed through the chaos of fun,
Just two rolling tumbleweeds, under the sun!

Each prick was a giggle, each poke a delight,
In the vicious embrace, we twirled through the night.
The barbs of our friendship, a comical war,
Dueling with laughter, we're never outscore.

So next time you hug, just be wary my friend,
A vicious embrace can be fun in the end.
In laughter's warm light, let's dance through the sting,
For love's just a prick, but it makes our hearts sing!

The Hardest Cuts of Truth

In a forest of fibs, where tall tales grow,
The weeds of wisdom seem to go slow.
But watch your step, for close at hand,
The truth is standing, quite unmanned.

With a snicker and grit, the whispers disclose,
How even the trickster sport a few woes.
A squirrel in a suit, oh what a sight,
Spilling secrets while munching on light!

The gossiping trees, with leaves all a-quiver,
Share stories of that one sneaky river.
It chuckles and flows, a true joker's flair,
Ripped from the roots, but none seem to care.

So gather around for a laugh with the spry,
Where truths leap about, and lies learn to fly.
In this wild charade, the punchlines abound,
The hardest cuts of truth, always found!

Sagas Beneath the Scrub

Beneath the thick brush, a tale starts to spin,
With critters debating, let the banter begin.
A hedgehog in boots and a wise old owl,
Plotting great mischief with a cheeky growl.

The snails set the pace, as they slip and slide,
While ants in their army muster with pride.
They strategize moves to steal all the crumbs,
While laughter erupts from the wise old bums.

A rabbit in jester's hat hops around,
Cracking up the crowd with jokes that astound.
"Why did the berry refuse to go home?
Because it got lost in the wild in its foam!"

So let's raise a toast to the sagas we tell,
Of mischief and mirth, where all creatures dwell.
Beneath the thick scrub, where humor ignites,
Each story a chuckle, by day and by nights!

Echoes of the Enchanted Wild

In the echoes of laughter through woodland corridors,
The owls hold debates, while the fox giggles more.
A party of shadows is gathered to dance,
With bees that bumble and squirrels that prance.

"Did you hear the one about the fish that could fly?
It flopped on a twig and yelled out, 'Oh my!'
They say it was caught, still swimming in dreams,
Riding on rafts made of riverbed beams."

A frog in a crown claims the throne of the bog,
Polishing his rule on a gem of a log.
With quips and quibbles, his subjects all cheer,
The monarch of mirth has made laughter near!

In this wild enchantment, where tales jig and jive,
Every rustle and whisper, keeps humor alive.
Among the green giants, let joy be compiled,
Echoes that linger of the enchanted wild!

From the Depths of Dark Woods

In dark woods where shadows and mischief entwine,
The owls plot nonsense; it's their prime design.
A blunder from bats, who can't navigate,
Tangled in twigs, oh, what a sad fate!

The rabbit reveals his latest fiasco,
Tripped over his ears while fleeing a cat, though.
As squirrels provide commentary on the side,
With nut-cracking laughter as their boundless guide.

Creatures unite for a wild concert night,
The raccoon on drums means we're in for a fright.
Though off-beat and silly, the chorus takes flight,
In the depths of dark woods, it's pure delight!

So let's celebrate gags in the thick of the gloom,
Where punchlines like mushrooms rise after the bloom.
In this forest of laughter, we dance and we play,
Turning frowns upside down, come what may!

The Duality of Bloom

In a garden so bright, blooms giggle and sway,
Yet one plant is grumpy, just ruining the play.
With petals like laughter, it dances with glee,
While the thorny one pouts, "Why can't they see me?"

The daisies throw parties, with polka-dot cheer,
While the rose sulks alone, nursing its beer.
A bud starts to blossom, with followers bold,
But oh! That thorn whispers, "Don't trust what you're told!"

In a patch full of joy, humor sprouts all around,
But hidden beneath, a wild rumor is found.
The happy blooms chatter of sunshine so bright,
While the prickly one scowls, "I'll ruin your night!"

So let's raise a toast to this quirky bouquet,
Where giggles are plenty, and thorns can't dismay.
For even the prickles, in their grumpy old way,
Find fun in their chaos and join in the play.

Fencelines of the Heart

On a fence made of whispers, two hearts play a game,
One blossoms like sunshine, the other's quite lame.
"I'm happy," says Daisy, with a smile so bright,
While Grumpy Old Thorn retorts, "I'll ruin your night!"

With jokes that fall flat and laughter that stings,
They bicker like siblings, and oh, how it swings!
Daisy shares secrets, soft petals laid bare,
While Thorn rolls its eyes, "Please, just go elsewhere!"

But one sunny morning, a giggle escapes,
From the prickly old fencer, emerging from shapes.
With laughter like rain, they both start to bloom,
Proving even the thorns can shake off their gloom.

Now fencelines of laughter stretch wide through the field,

Where hearts intertwine, and the best is revealed.
For sometimes the prickle, though steely and harsh,
Can spark the connection for a joyful new march.

Stories of the Untamed

Beneath the wild chaos, there's mischief galore,
Where tales of the untamed shake off every lore.
A daisy pulls pranks on an unsuspecting bee,
While a thorny old bramble just waits patiently.

"Oh, tell me a story!" the butterflies tease,
As they flutter and giggle, wrapped up in a breeze.
But thorny just huffs, "I've got tales of my own,
Like how to trip daisies and claim the throne!"

One day comes a spider with plans quite absurd,
It weaves a fine web and calls it a word.
"Gather 'round, friends! Let's spin tales that amaze!"
But thorn swipes its claws, "I'll just add my malaise!"

Yet stories of laughter, in this wild bloom fest,
Show thorns can be funny, they're odd but the best.
So burrow in tightly, let chaos ignite,
For amidst all the mayhem, pure joy takes flight.

In the Midst of Thorns

In a patch of wild laughter, thorns stand up tall,
Wearing prickles like armor, yet craving a ball.
"Why don't you join us?" calls a soft petaled friend,
But the thorns just chuckle, "We'd rather offend!"

"Oh dear," sighs the daisy, with a twinkle and spin,
"Can't you see, dear old thorn, where the humor begins?"

Yet thorny just grins, with a glint in its eye,
"I'll be here to poke fun, with a bit of a sly."

As bumbles and giggles twirl round in delight,
The thorn cracks a joke and it takes off in flight.
With a burst of pure laughter, it joins in the fray,
Proving blushing blooms need a prankster each day.

So in the midst of thorns, where giggles soar high,
Nothing's as funny as friends saying "Oh my!"
For every sharp edge brings a laugh, it seems clear,
That humor's the magic that blooms year to year.

The Boughs of Burden

In a forest where laughter wears hats,
Branches giggle like mischievous cats.
They stumble and wiggle, oh such a sight,
Even the owls roll their eyes at the flight.

Boughs bowed down with berries and woes,
Caterpillars dance in comical rows.
With nectar so sweet, the bees start to hum,
Calling the ants to come join the fun.

A squirrel leaps high with a nut in his grip,
But lands on a branch that gives him a slip.
He spins like a top in the freshness of air,
Spreading joy, for he hasn't a care.

So come take a stroll where the boughs do bend,
And laugh at the scenes that nature can send.
For in this wild place where burdens grow light,
There's humor in thorns that tickle and bite.

A Dance with the Bramble

Bramble bushes twist like a waltzing pair,
With leaps and with bounds, they dance with the air.
But watch where you step, and keep your shoes tight,
For they'll grab at your socks, if you're not quite right.

With each little poke, the brambles all cheer,
"Come take part in our ball! We're glad you are here!"
A rabbit hops in, but soon finds his fate,
Stuck tangled in laughter, it seems quite a state.

An acorn rolls by, as if in a chase,
With giggles and wiggles, it joins in the race.
The hedgehogs all snicker and roll on the ground,
"Who knew that the bramble would dance all around?"

So leap with the laughter, oh twirl and collide,
In the dance of the bramble, let joy be your guide.
For every sharp poke just adds to the thrill,
A twist and a turn, there's magic until.

Beneath the Boughs of Brambles

Beneath the thick branches where shadows do play,
Lies a stage for the critters at the end of the day.
With tangles and bickering, who's in the right,
They argue and chirp, what a comical sight!

The rabbits debate on the fastest of routes,
While squirrels argue cheese, and what makes it sprout.
"Is it the dance or the wiggle?" They muse,
As ants scribble notes, all seeking to choose.

With whispers of dreams that float like a breeze,
The butterflies giggle, hoping to tease.
A hedgehog proclaims with a puffed-out cheer,
"Life's riddled with quirks that we hold so dear!"

So joining the banter, the laughter rolls free,
For beneath the brambles, it's nonsense, you see!
With giggling branches that tickle the ground,
In this wild little world, joy can be found.

The Hidden Edge of Kindness

In a patch where the prickers make homes for the meek,
Lies a treasure of kindness for those who dare seek.
With raspberries grinning, they wave as you pass,
While the dandelions gossip about the soft grass.

A porcupine's smile is an awkward delight,
For his quills tell tales of how he puts up a fight.
Yet deep in his heart, a softie resides,
Behind those sharp edges, sweet love still abides.

The bumbles buzz round in a curious trance,
As they trip on the roots that invite them to dance.
And even the thorns that prick at your skin,
Hold stories of laughter, let the fun begin!

So wander on softly, with kindness in tow,
For in every prickle, there's more room to grow.
With a giggle and wink, let your heart come alive,
In this curious place where the kindest thrive.

Tales from the Prickled Path

In a garden where roses grow,
I met a squirrel who stole the show.
He wore a hat made of leaves and twine,
Claimed it was fashion, truly divine.

His friends joined in, all decked in green,
Dancing around like a silly scene.
With a laugh and a wiggle, they'd trip and fall,
Each landing with jokes that cracked us all.

But one little pup, full of sass,
Thought the roses were meant to pass.
He dashed through the thorns, oh what a display,
Came back with blooms, with a thorny bouquet!

So off they pranced, with prickers galore,
Laughing at life, forever wanting more.
'Tales from the garden,' they'd proudly shout,
'Of pricks and of prickles, let's dance about!'

The Grit of Growth

There once was a cactus named Sam,
Who dreamed of being a soft little ham.
He dressed up in cotton, oh so absurd,
Hoping to blend in with the birds.

But the birds all laughed, they said with a tweet,
'Sam, you're a prickly little treat!'
He puffed out his chest, said, 'I'm proud of my spines,
I make tacos complete, those are my designs!'

Then one sunny day, they threw a big feast,
With salsa and guac, oh what a beast.
Sam showed up gleaming, embracing his flair,
No longer shamed, he flaunted with care.

Now each time they gather, a toast they all raise,
To grit and to growth, to hands full of praise.
For who could resist such a spiky delight,
Bringing laughter and joy all through the night?

Wounds that Blossom

There was a young rose with a passion to grow,
She fancied her petals more vibrant than show.
But oh, the poor thing, she stumbled and fell,
Got stuck on a branch, like a thorny carousel.

Her friends came to help, giggly and close,
With a rope made of stems, they plotted, you know.
'We're in this together, it's all in good fun!'
With a push and a pull, they cheered 'we're not done!'

Out popped the rose, with a flourish and spin,
Covered in dirt, what a mess she was in.
Yet laughter erupted, she giggled so bright,
'Next time I'll watch where I take my first flight!'

And now every spring, they make a big fuss,
Out on the lawn, they laugh, sing, and thus,
Blooming together, their bond now so strong,
In wounds they found laughter, where they all belong.

Ensnared by Vines

A vine one day sang a whimsical tune,
Claiming it caught every flower at noon.
But a daisy named Sue, with a wild little shout,
Said, 'You'd be surprised what I can pull out!'

With a flick of her petals, oh what a jive,
She twisted and twirled, kept her bloom alive.
The vine just chuckled, replied with a grin,
'You call that a dance? Here, let me begin!'

So they battled it out, a contest of cheer,
The garden now buzzing, as the critters drew near.
With each graceful step, they wrapped all around,
Creating a tangle, oh joyously bound.

In the end, they found laughter in strife,
Forever entangled, they danced through life.
Two friends in a twist, what a sight to behold,
In vines and in petals, both lively and bold!

A Rose in the Rough

In a garden where the laughter blooms,
A hedgehog wore a floral costume.
The bees threw a party, a buzzing delight,
But danced on the petals, oh what a sight!

A snail slid in, thinking he could glide,
Tripped on a stem, then tried to hide.
The roses all giggled, they knew he would fall,
In this quirky patch, there's humor for all.

With thorns in the bushes and jokes in the air,
A bumblebee juggled, without any care.
"Take a bow," he buzzed, as petals unfurled,
In a garden of laughs, let joy be twirled!

Even daisies chimed in with a punchline or two,
As raindrops tapped lightly, their skies never blue.
For a rose in the rough knows just how to cheer,
With laughter as lovely as petals appear!

Fables from the Bramble

In a bramble where no one dared to roam,
A rabbit told tales of his faraway home.
He spoke of a fox who wore shoes of straw,
And danced on his toes, what a funny flaw!

The vines served as chairs for a council of bugs,
They sipped on sweet nectar and shared silly hugs.
A ladybug laughed, "It's all in the grind,
And if you ask nicely, I'll drop you a rind."

A sassy old tortoise, with wisdom so grand,
Said, "Speed is overrated, just take your stand!"
With stories all twisted, and humor entwined,
Fables from thorns were not hard to find.

A crow landed softly, with jokes in his beak,
He cawed, "Why sit still when we could take a peek?"
With laughter a-plenty, they forgot about fright,
In the bramble, they played until the night!

Secrets Among the Spines

In books on a shelf, where the stories confide,
Lived a wise old cactus who swelled with pride.
"Dear reader," he whispered, "I've secrets to share,
But watch for the prickle, and handle with care!"

A porcupine poet recited with flair,
Lines of sharp humor that tickled the air.
"Why don't the cacti ever get a date?
They're too prickly to hug, oh, isn't that fate?"

Their laughter rumbled through pages and spine,
For in this old library, humor was fine.
A flower in the windows, with petals so bright,
Said, "Let's sprinkle some love to take flight tonight!"

With giggles and snickers, they shared out their tales,
Of friendships and mishaps, of ships with no sails.
Secrets among spines, oh, such joyful sights,
In this whimsical world, where laughter ignites!

The Edge of Sorrow

In a field where sadness seemed to sit tight,
A scarecrow joked, "Let me show you the light!"
With a hat that was crooked, and boots made of hay,
He spun tales of joy, making gloom fade away.

The daisies chimed in, all dressed in white,
"Who needs heavy hearts when we can take flight?"
A bumblebee buzzed, "Let's paint the town bright,
With colors of laughter, we'll dance through the night!"

From gloomy to goofy, the shift was profound,
As smiles emerged, and joy spun around.
"Why cry at the thorns, when petals are near?
Let's laugh at the troubles, and celebrate cheer!"

So on the edge of sorrow, they clutched at the fun,
In fields of resilience, they danced in the sun.
For even in shadows, where whispers may dwell,
The heart finds its giggle, a secret to tell!

Lost in the Tangle

In a garden of snags, I lost my way,
Dancing with nettles, oh, what a display.
A squirrel laughed loud, it fell off its branch,
I tripped on a vine, then joined the big dance.

I waved to the thorns, they waved back with sparks,
Poking and prodding, like playful sharks.
A picnic of giggles, a feast of the weird,
Got stuck in the bush, now I'm slightly beard.

Each step was a grab, like a game of escape,
Raccoons were my judges, in leafy drape.
With every odd twist, I spun like a top,
The sun at high noon said, "Oh, make it stop!"

But here in the mess, I found joy today,
In prickly confusion, I dance and I sway.
Life's tangled up moments can sting, it is true,
But laughter's a balm; how we grew and we grew!

Bark and Bloom

A tree with a grin, bark covered in jokes,
Whispering stories to the cartoon folks.
Buds full of giggles, blossoms that snort,
In the wacky orchard, I found a new sport.

Bees in the branches, doing a dance,
Buzzing around with a quirky romance.
They mixed up the nectar, changed it to tea,
Served with a side of sweet comedy.

Rabbits in capes wore hats made of leaves,
Spinning tall tales right under the eaves.
Each bloom held a chuckle, each vine held a sigh,
Garden of giggles beneath the bright sky.

So come take a cheer, embrace the absurd,
Every odd twist is a tale to be heard.
In bark and in bloom, let your laughter resume,
In nature's funny fit, let the madness consume!

The Webb of Bristling Stories

In a web spun of laughter, I found my sweet place,
Caught up in the chuckles, a funny little race.
The spider eyed me with a grin so wide,
Spinning tall tales from the yarn of my pride.

A caterpillar strolled, wearing shoes so bright,
Wobbling along, giving all such a fright.
He flipped through the pages of a leaf-covered book,
With each little jab, it had me all shook.

With bristles and giggles, they spun quite the yarn,
Mice joined the circus; they danced on the lawn.
The tales of the night were full of delight,
As shadows went creeping, we laughed till we'd cry.

In this web of stories, I found a great friend,
With whimsy and mischief that'd never quite end.
Let's revel in quirks that life has in store,
For laughter and tales are what we adore!

Secrets Between the Sharp

In a thicket of secrets, I tripped on a block,
Met a wise old owl who just loved to mock.
"Tell me your tale," he hooted with glee,
As he juggled some berries still stuck to a tree.

Prickly and funny, the stories unfurled,
Squirrels played poker; the stakes had been swirled.
Tails high in the air, they'd bluff with pure grace,
While the hedgehogs would giggle and roll in the space.

A lizard cut loose with a dance on a stone,
Said, "Life's just a play, and we're never alone!"
With quills raised in laughter, they formed a parade,
As secrets between sharp things made the day fade.

So let's raise a laugh where the sharp things do dwell,
For each hidden tale, we can share with a yell.
In the garden of giggles, we'll find a delight,
With secrets and laughter, we'll dance through the night!

Prickles of Memory

In the garden of jokes, we plant a seed,
With laughter so bright, it's hard to mislead.
Yet memories poke like a playful tease,
Each prick brings a smile, oh, if you please!

A tale of a hedgehog, slick and sly,
Who tried to fly high with a kite in the sky.
Yet tangled in twine, what a spin he made,
Now he tells friends, 'I'm just well displayed!'

The cactus in the corner, with arms open wide,
Played peek-a-boo every time we'd slide.
We'd laugh and we'd giggle, each tumble a show,
While the cactus just sat, wearing pride, don't you know?

So here's to our stories, with pricks all around,
They keep us from floating too high off the ground.
For life's a grand garden, with blooms and with thorns,
And every small jab makes our laughter reborn.

The Briar's Whisper

In the thicket of tales, a briar did speak,
With whispers of mischief, a giggle unique.
He told of a rabbit who danced with a shoe,
And wore it all day, yelling, 'Look at my view!'

A squirrel wanted nuts, as they often do,
But tripped on a log, made a comical brew.
As he rolled down the hill, in a whirl of delight,
He shouted, 'I'm winning! Call it a night!'

The briar chuckled, 'Oh, the folly I've seen,
From the prattling hedgehogs to the ants so keen.
Each slip and each fall brings a smile to my spine,
In this forest of mishaps, oh how we shine!'

So when you move near, don't just rush on by,
Listen to whispers that dance in the sky.
For laughter is blooming where prickles reside,
In the tangled up stories, let humor be your guide.

Unfolding in Shadows

When shadows grow long, and stories unfold,
We gather our giggles, and soon they are told.
Of a pinecone who fancied himself quite a star,
He rolled with the wind, but didn't get far!

Around him would flutter the leaves in dismay,
As they whispered, 'Dear pinecone, you're in our way!'
But he laughed in the breeze, with a twirl and a spin,
'If you can't take me down, then let's all dive in!'

In the dusk of the forest, where shadows play tricks,
A porcupine's joke makes the brambles do flips.
He said, 'I'm quite prickly, but don't take offense,
For behind these sharp quills lies a soft pretense!'

So gather your tales from the edge of the woods,
Where the prickers and ticklers wear friendship like hoods.
And in every shadow, a laugh you may find,
Where prickly to funny, oh, how we're entwined!

Petals of Resilience

In the flower patch bright, where humor takes root,
A daisy with dreams spoke up, 'Isn't it cute?'
She tugged on her petals, shaped funny and round,
'Life's never a burden when joy can be found!'

A marigold chimed in, with curls like a star,
'We bloom with a giggle, no matter where we are!'
Together they danced, on a breeze oh so light,
Making jokes with each petal, in the soft morning light.

But watch out for bees, with their buzzing parade,
They swarm with their laughter, no need for afraid.
For even the buzzing brings petals a cheer,
'Join us in fun, there's nothing to fear!'

So let us be flowers, with humor our guide,
Through sunshine and shadows, we'll bloom side by side.

With resilience like petals, our laughter will thrive,
In a world full of prickers, together we'll strive!

The Rose's Painful Embrace

In the garden where roses grow,
A bee got caught in a thorny show.
He buzzed and he whined, what a silly plight,
While petals giggled, it was quite a sight.

The roses conspired to have some fun,
Telling the bee, 'You can't outrun!
With each little poke, you learn a new trick,
But oh dear bee, you sure are thick!'

A butterfly landed, with laughter so bright,
'You're stuck like a joke in a springtime fight!'
The flowers all chimed in a playful cheer,
'Next time, dear bee, stay far from here!'

So the garden now tells of that day so grand,
Of a bee's antics and thorns so unplanned.
In a world full of beauty, with laughter abound,
Even prickly little things can turn life around.

Fables in the Underbrush

In the thicket so thick, where laughter swells,
Lived a family of brambles with stories to tell.
A fox passed by, with a curious glance,
He'd heard of their fables, oh, what a chance!

'Gather 'round, friends!' cried the leader of knits,
'Our tales are sharp, like our prickly bits!
There once was a crow who loved shiny things,
Till he tangled his wings in our spiky slings!'

The hedgehogs chuckled, 'Now that's just bald!
He learned not to hoard what the brambles had scrawled.
Every shiny object has its wily cost,
For in mishaps like his, your glitter gets lost!'

So the fables flew high, on wings made of mirth,
In the underbrush hide, where the funny takes birth.
With every new story, they danced and they spun,
In a world full of laughter, even danger is fun!

Echoes Among the Thickets

Echoes ring out through the lush, leafy maze,
Where the critters all giggle in sunshine's warm blaze.
They gather their tales under branches so wide,
Where mischief and laughter are always allied.

A squirrel once claimed he could leap like a bird,
But tangled in bushes, he broke his own word.
With thorns in his fur and a frown on his face,
He chattered, 'Next time, I'd prefer some more space!'

The bunnies all cackled, with giggling glee,
'Your bravado's a joke, oh, can't you see?
It's not fame or triumph that fills up our spots,
But the laughter we share and the fun we have got!'

So echoes now linger, with stories so fine,
In thickets where laughter and whimsy combine.
For each little mishap is a treasure we make,
In the wild, joyful tales only time can mistake.

The Beauty That Bites

In a garden where beauty seems never to fade,
A flower with charm had a mischievous blade.
While admirers would stop to marvel and sigh,
They'd find out too late, beauty isn't so shy!

'What a stunning bloom!' cried the giddy young lass,
As she reached out to touch, oh, what a faux pas!
The flower giggled, 'Take care, little dear,
I charm and I bite, now shed not a tear!'

The petals would wave, like they're holding a show,
But the moment you venture, it's a ticket to woe.
So beware of the flowers with beauty that calls,
For one unexpected prick can lead to some falls!

So the garden now sings of its comical spree,
Of the beauty that bites, yes, oh can't you see?
In a world full of laughter and petals so fair,
Sometimes it's the prickles that bring out the flair!

Underneath the Green Enigma

In the garden, a riddle grew,
With leafy whispers and a clue.
I tripped on roots and went for a dive,
Who knew plants could make me jive?

Jelly beans sprouted, I grabbed a fist,
But found a bug that made me twist.
The color was bold, the flavor a prank,
Spicy surprise gave my tongue a crank!

The flowers laughed, they watched my flair,
As bees all buzzed, giving me a scare.
With laughter erupted from every sprout,
Who knew veggies could throw such clout?

The sun set low, the shadows long,
A jester's cap on the frog's old song.
I skipped away, my harvest a tease,
In the garden of giggles, I did as I please.

The Price of Sweetness

In a world where candy grows,
Chasing sugar led to woes.
I spotted lollipops, so bright and round,
But sticky sap had my shoes all bound.

The gumball tree waved with glee,
I marched right up, so bold and free.
But a cheeky squirrel claimed his claim,
He threw a nut—oh, what a game!

With every bite of candied loot,
Came a dash of berry, then a fruit.
But rind and vinegar all morphed together,
"Guess I'll wear this on a sweater!"

As I shuffled home, a sugar-laden mess,
I laughed aloud at my own silly stress.
For in the chase, the sweet and wild,
Life's a party, just like a child.

Berries and Brambles

In a patch where berries danced and played,
I stumbled in, quite unafraid.
With every berry that caught my eye,
A hidden bramble made me cry!

The blue ones winked as I drew near,
But sharp little hooks made it clear.
I thought I'd win at berry pie,
Instead, I left with a giant sigh.

A friendly hedgehog offered a hand,
"Join my team! We'll berry-band!"
We rolled and tumbled, oh what a race,
But trip on a bramble? That's bad news face!

In the end, we laughed as we picked in jest,
With each mishap, I felt truly blessed.
Though berries twinkled and called my name,
The brambles joked, "You're part of our game!"

Love Wrapped in Prickles

A cactus stood, all spiky and proud,
Declared, "I'm the love of the crowd!"
But every kind gesture it made with glee,
Left a tiny mark on my unsuspecting knee!

The roses, too with their petals so bright,
Gave me a hug, and oh, what a fright!
With love like a thorn, I laughed till I cried,
Was this the romance the poets had tried?

Each little bloom had its tricks in store,
Inviting sweet laughter and prickles galore.
But in every pinch, I saw the fun,
Even a cactus can't stop love on the run.

So here's to romance, both sweet and strange,
With all of its quirks and wild exchanges.
For in every laugh and each tender nip,
Lies the beauty of love, in a silly script!

www.ingramcontent.com/pod-product-compliance
Lightning Source LLC
Chambersburg PA
CBHW071822160426
43209CB00003B/176